Hippos

Hippos

Jenny Markert

THE CHILD'S WORLD®, INC.

Published in the United States of America by The Child's World®, Inc.
PO Box 326
Chanhassen, MN 55317-0326
800-599-READ
www.childsworld.com

Product Manager Mary Berendes
Editor Katherine Stevenson
Designer Mary Berendes
Contributor Bob Temple

Photo Credits
ANIMALS ANIMALS © Anup Shah: 26
ANIMALS ANIMALS © Bruce Davidson: 2
ANIMALS ANIMALS © Dani/Jeske: 10
ANIMALS ANIMALS © Pooley, H. OSF: 24
© 1996 Anup Shah/Dembinsky Photo Assoc. Inc.: 20
© 2000 Anup Shah/Dembinsky Photo Assoc. Inc.: cover, 23
© Art Wolfe, The National Audubon Society Collection/Photo Researchers: 6
© Daniel J. Cox/naturalexposures.com: 19
© 2000 Fritz Polking/Dembinsky Photo Assoc. Inc.: 29
© Gerald & Buff Corsi/Visuals Unlimited: 13
© 1995 Kevin Schafer: 9
© 1998 Kevin Schafer: 16
© Lynne Ledbetter/Visuals Unlimited: 15
© 2001 Manoj Shah/Stone: 30

Library of Congress Cataloging-in-Publication Data
Markert, Jenny.
Hippos / by Jenny Markert.
p. cm.
Includes index.
ISBN 1-56766-880-1 (library bound : alk. paper)
1. Hippopotamus—Juvenile literature. [1. Hippopotamus.]
I.Title.
QL737.U57 M37 2001
599.63'5—dc21
00-010780

On the cover...

Front cover: This adult hippo is swimming in Tanzania.
Page 2: From close up, you can see that this hippo is sweating.

Table of Contents

The water in the African water hole is smooth and still. Flies buzz at the muddy edges, and birds chirp softly in the air. Suddenly two eyes, two ears, and a big nose peek out above the murky water. The rest of the animal's body is hidden underwater. The animal moves closer to land. With a loud splash, this huge creature plows out of the water and charges onto the shore. What is this giant creature? It's a hippopotamus!

What Are Hippopotamuses?

Hippopotamuses are **mammals.** Mammals are animals that have hair or fur and feed their babies milk from their bodies. People, cows, and monkeys are mammals, too. Hippos have just a tiny bit of hair on their faces, backs, and tails. Because hippopotamuses have such a long name, we call them "hippos" for short.

This huge hippo is wading in water that is covered with weeds. ⇒

Are There Different Kinds of Hippos?

There are two kinds of hippopotamuses. The most common type is the large *river hippo*. River hippos are the kind most people see in zoos and pictures. The second type is the smaller *pygmy hippo*. Both river hippos and pygmy hippos live in Africa. They spend much of their time in lakes, rivers, and water holes. The water keeps the animals cool and protects their skin from sunburn.

⇐ This adult pygmy hippo is looking for some grasses to eat.

What Do Hippos Look Like?

Hippos can grow very large. Male river hippos stand up to five feet high at their shoulders and weigh about 8,000 pounds! Hippos have small ears and small tails. They also have large eyes near the top of their head. Their eyes help them see above the water while the rest of their body stays underwater.

Hippos have gray or brown skin that they must protect from the sun. Without water, their skin would quickly dry out and crack. To help keep their skin wet, hippos sweat a pinkish liquid that looks a little like blood.

It is easy to see this hippo's large body ⇒
as it stands on the shore in Kenya.

Do Hippos Swim?

Hippos don't really swim. Instead, they walk on the bottoms of rivers and lakes. Using their powerful legs, the hippos push off the bottom and bounce slowly along. When they go underwater, their ears and noses close tightly to keep the water out. Hippos can stay under for about six minutes before coming up for air. That's a long time to hold your breath!

These two hippos are walking underwater at the San Diego Zoo. ⇒

What Do Hippos Eat?

Hippos are **herbivores,** which means that they eat only plants. To hippos, the bottom of a river or lake is like a dinner table. They find many types of underwater weeds and other plants they like to eat. Hippos spend much of their day finding these green underwater plants and munching them slowly. Then they often take a nap—sometimes underwater!

⇐ Here you can see an adult hippo peeking
out from some floating weeds.

Even though they live mostly in the water, hippos love to eat one food that grows on land—grass. The hippos wait until late in the day, or even until nighttime. When they feel safe, they come out of the water and graze on grass growing nearby. Since hippos are so big, they need a lot of food. An adult hippo can eat 300 pounds of grass and other plants in a single day!

You can see inside this hippo's mouth as it ⇒ feeds on grasses near Kenya's Mara River.

Hippos live in groups called **herds.** Each herd usually has between 6 and 15 members. Herds include a **creche** (KRESH), which is like a childcare center for hippos. A creche is made up of female hippos, called **cows,** and their babies, called **calves.** The cows decide where the herd makes its home. Usually they choose the bank of a river or lake.

Hippos are usually friendly and sociable with each other. They huddle close together when they sleep, sometimes even using each other as pillows.

⟸ Most of the hippos in this Kenyan herd are sleeping. Two have found a spot on a sunny rock.

Do Hippos Fight?

Male hippos are called **bulls.** Normally, they don't live with the females and young hippos. Instead, they claim areas called **territories** near the herd and help protect the creche. Each bull defends its territory and doesn't allow other bulls near. If a bull goes into another bull's territory, there is usually a fight.

These two bulls are fighting in the Mara River. ⇒

Before fighting, a bull hippo tries to scare the intruder away. He bellows and roars, opening his mouth as wide as possible. A hippo's jaws can open four feet wide—big enough to hold several basketballs! Inside are four large teeth called **tusks.** They are a little like an elephant's tusks, only smaller. Hippos also have large, sharp teeth called **incisors.** If neither bull backs down, the two bite and slash each other with their teeth. Sometimes they fight until one of the hippos dies.

Hippo cows give birth to only one calf at a time. The calves are born in the water. They are safer there than on land. Newborn hippo calves are big—between 60 and 100 pounds! Once the calf is born, it rises to the surface and takes its first breath. Its mother stays with it and cares for it. Within days, the young calf is running, swimming, and getting to know the other hippos.

← This little calf is playing near its mother.

Do Hippos Have Enemies?

Adult hippos have very few enemies. What animal would want to attack something that is so huge and has such big teeth? Young hippos aren't as safe as their parents. Lions, leopards, wild dogs, and crocodiles sometimes catch and eat calves that wander away from the herd. A calf's tough skin protects it against cuts and scrapes, but only an adult hippo can save it from a hungry enemy.

Here a young hippo is investigating a crocodile. If the hippo ⇒ gets too close, the crocodile may snap its powerful jaws.

When you glimpse the top of a hippo's head on the surface of the water, it's hard to believe what is hidden below. Imagine such a huge body walking along the bottom, with only its eyes peeking above the surface. The next time you go swimming, think about the hippopotamus. Be glad you're not swimming in an African water hole—and that hippos prefer to munch on grass rather than toes!

Glossary

bulls (BULLZ)
Male hippos are called bulls. Bull hippos sometimes fight each other.

calves (KAVZ)
Baby hippos are called calves. Hippo calves are born in the water.

cows (KOWZ)
Female hippos are called cows. A hippo cow gives birth to only one baby at a time.

creche (KRESH)
A creche is a group of female and baby hippos. The creche helps keep the baby hippos safe.

herbivores (HER-bih-vorz)
Herbivores are animals that eat only plants. Hippos are herbivores.

herds (HERDZ)
Herds are groups of animals that live together. Hippos live in herds.

incisors (in-SY-zerz)
Incisors are sharp front teeth that are used for cutting. Male hippos bite with their incisors when they fight.

mammals (MAM-mullz)
Mammals are animals that have warm blood, have hair on their bodies, and produce milk to feed their babies. Hippos are mammals, and so are people.

territories (TEHR-ih-tor-eez)
Territories are areas that animals claim as their own. Male hippos have territories they defend against other males.

tusks (TUSKS)
Tusks are very large teeth. Hippos' tusks are not as big as elephant tusks.

Web Sites

http://sailfish.exis.net/~spook/hipptxt.html

http://library.thinkquest.org/16645/wildlife/hippopotamus.shtml

http://www.pbs.org/kratts/world/africa/hippo/index.html

Index